AF394812

First published in 2023 by:

Northern Eye Books Limited

Northern Eye Books, Tattenhall, Cheshire CH3 9PX

© Northern Eye Books Limited 2023

ISBN 978-1-914589-15-7

Text: Julia Goodfellow-Smith

Series editor: Tony Bowerman

Photographs: Julia Goodfellow-Smith, Crown copyright (2023) Visit Wales, Alamy, Adobe Stock, Dreamstime, Shutterstock

Design: Carl Rogers and Laura Hodgkinson

www.northerneyebooks.co.uk

www.walescoastpath.co.uk

@northerneyebooks
@wales_coast_path
@juliagsauthorspeaker

@northerneyeboo
@WalesCoastUK

@northerneyebooks
@wales_coast_path
@juliagsauthor

For sales enquiries, please call 01928 723 744
tony@northerneyebooks.co.uk

Cover: *Beer garden overlooking Rhossili Bay, Gower (Walk 4)*

6. Turn left onto the track, then after 30-40 metres where there's a junction with a series of signposts, turn right following Wales Coast Path signs. Follow this track as it wends its way round to a tarmac lane.

Turn left here for the visitor centre, or right to return to the car park. ♦

Newport Wetlands Nature Reserve

The installation of the Cardiff Bay barrage destroyed a lot of valuable wildlife habitat. To offset some of the losses, this site was transformed from an industrial and farming wasteland into a thriving bird reserve managed by the RSPB. The reedbeds here provide the only successful breeding site in Wales for bitterns and bearded tits, and this is the best place in South Wales to see murmurations of starlings in winter.

Useful Information

Wales Coast Path

Comprehensive information and maps for all sections of the Wales Coast Path can be found at www.walescoastpath.gov.uk. See also www.walescoastpath.co.uk

Visit South Wales

The South Wales official tourism website covers everything from accommodation and special events to attractions and adventure. www.visitwales.com/explore/south-wales. For other areas, see: www.visitwales.com/info/tourist-information-across-wales

South Wales breweries and pubs

Oddly enough, it was the Sunday Closing Act of 1881 that helped shape Wales' unique 'Welshness', and it was only in 1996 that the last district, Dwyfor, abandoned 'Dry Sundays'. Before that, not a drop was drunk legally in Wales on the Sabbath.

Today, the southern half of Wales boasts both mainstream breweries like Brain's and Rhymney, and a growing number of regional microbreweries that include Tiny Rebel and Flowerhorn (Cardiff), Tomos Watkin and Drop Bear (Swansea), and Bluestone Brewing and Tenby Brewery (Pembrokeshire).

For details of the encouragingly high number of real ale pubs across South Wales, see the local CAMRA websites, or buy a copy of their excellent, annual **Good Beer Guide**.

Visitors can also sample many of the mouth-watering Welsh beers and ciders at festivals that include the Gower Beer Festival (June), Swansea Bay Beer and Cider Festival (August), Cardiff Brewfest (August), and Carmarthen Beer Festival (October).

Weather

Online weather forecasts for the South Wales coast are available from the Met Office at www.metoffice.gov.uk

Contents

Rhayader
Aberaeron
New Quay
CEREDIGION
Tregaron
Llandrindod
Wells
Kington
Synod Inn
Builth
Wells
Lampeter
HEREFO
Cardigan
Pumsaint
Llanwrtyd
Wells
Hay-
on-Wye
Here
Newcastle
Emlyn
Fishguard
Crymych
Llandovery
Brecon
Talgarth
Cynwyl
Elfed
CARMARTHENSHIRE
Llangadog
Sennybridge
BLAENAU
GWENT
Crickhowell
Davids
PEMBROKESHIRE
Llandeilo
BRECON BEACONS
Carmarthen
MERTHYR
TYDFIL
Abergaver
rfordwest
Narberth
St Clears
Brynamman
Merthyr
Tydfil
Monm
Milford
Haven
Pembroke
Dock
Ammanford
Kidwelly
Ebbw
Vale
MONMOUTH
Pembroke
Penaine
Llanelli
Aberdare
Pontypool
Usk
Tenby
Carmarthen
Bay
SWANSEA
NEATH
PORT TALBOT
Treorchy
Cwmbran
Che
St Govan's
Head
Swansea
Neath
Maesteg
Caerphilly
Gowe
Worms Head/
Penrhyn-Gŵyr
Port
Talbot
Pontypridd
wport
Port-Eynon
Swansea
Bay
Bridgend
CARDIFF
Avonm
Porthcawl
VALE OF
GLAMORGAN
Clevedon
Penarth
Cardiff-Wales
Airport
Barry
Weston-super-Mare
BRISTOL CHANNEL
Burnham-
on-Sea
Mend
Hills
Lundy
Lynton
Porlock
Minehead
Bridgwater Bay
Ilfracombe
North
Devon
EXMOOR
Glaston
Barnstaple
or
Bideford Bay
Braunton
Williton
Bridgwater
Quantock
Hills
SOME
Hartland Point
Northam
Taunton
Langport
Dulverton
Hartland
Bideford
South
Wellington

The Wales Coast Path

WALES IS THE ONLY COUNTRY IN THE WORLD with a path around its entire coast. The long-distance Wales Coast Path offers 870 miles/1400 kilometres of unbroken coastal walking, from the outskirts of the ancient walled city of Chester in the north to the Georgian market town of Chepstow in the south.

There's something new around every corner. Visually stunning and rich in both history and wildlife, the path promises ever-changing views, wildflowers and seabirds, as well as castles, coves and coastal pubs.

In fact, the Wales Coast Path runs through 1 Marine Nature Reserve, 2 National Parks, 3 Areas of Outstanding Natural Beauty, 11 National Nature Reserves, 14 Heritage Coasts, and 23 Historic Landscapes.

And, to cap it all, the **Wales Coast Path** links up with the long-distance Offa's Dyke Path at either end: creating a complete, 1,030 mile circuit of the whole of Wales.

Pretty Tenby is home to some great pubs and breweries

South Wales' coastal pubs

The South Wales coast is home to a surprising variety of beaches, coasts and historical sites. Rhossili Bay is battered by waves from the open Atlantic, while Laugharne and Llansteffan are sheltered by sandbanks. At Llantwit Major, the coast path lies atop limestone cliffs; at Nash, it is barely above sea level. Three walks skirt castles (Laugharne, Llansteffan and Cardiff) and both on the Gower visit Neolithic monuments. Habitats include dunes, wetlands, and 'Celtic rainforest'.

The pubs are equally varied, including a tap room in Tenby, a quirky modern bar in Cardiff, a community-owned pub in Nash and, of course, more traditional pubs and inns like those on the Gower. There really is something for everyone.

"I must go down to the seas again, for the call of the running tide, Is a wild call and a clear call that may not be denied"

— John Masefield, *Sea Fever*

TOP 10 Walks: South Wales' best coastal Pub Walks

EACH OF THESE CIRCULAR WALKS has been selected for both the quality of the pub and the walk itself. All are in landscapes with particular historical or wildlife interest, and all but one follow part of the coast path. That final walk runs parallel to the coast path at the top of the cliff, rather than the bottom.

These routes cover the very best walking country in the area. You may be surprised by the peace and beauty that can be found even in the more urban areas.

King Arthur Hotel
Reynoldston
page 30

The Woodman
PUB · DINING · GARDEN
Woodman
Black Pill.
page 36

Prince of Wales Inn
Kenfig
page 42

Old Swan Inn
Llantwit Major
page 48

Tiny Rebel
Tiny Rebel
Cardiff
page 54

Waterloo Inn
Nash Village
Newport.
page 58

The relaxed, modern bar at the Harbwr Tap

Harbwr Tap & Kitchen
Tenby

What to expect:
Easy walk with some elevation gain. Views over the harbour, town, and Carmarthen Bay

Distance/time: 6.5 kilometres / 4 miles. Allow 2½ hours

Start: North Bay car park (charges)

Grid ref: SN 134 011

Ordnance Survey map: Outdoor Leisure 36, *South Pembrokeshire*

The Pub: Harbwr Tap & Kitchen, Sergeant's Lane, St Julian St, Tenby SA70 7BU | 01834 842273 | www.harbwr.wales

Walk outline: A picturesque walk taking in the delights of the colourful seaside town of Tenby. After visiting the harbour, offering views of Carmarthen Bay and Caldey Island and passing through one of the gates into the walled town, the route follows a shaded path inland before turning back towards the sea and a beautiful hidden gem of a beach.

The Harbwr Tap & Kitchen is situated over the five-barrel craft brewery. Ask nicely, and you might even get to meet the head brewer. There are three spacious rooms and a sundeck with conservatory and shelter in case of Wales' infamous 'liquid sunshine'. Some of the Welsh rugby team reputedly drink here, so keep your eyes peeled.

Dogs are welcome

▶ The Harbwr Tap & Kitchen at a glance

Open: Daily from 10.30 am
Brewery/company: Harbwr
Ales and wine: Focus on beers brewed on-site
Food: Locally sourced, including seafood. 12-8 pm Mon-Sat, 12-5 pm Sun
Accommodation: None
Outside: A rooftop garden and shady tables in Sergeant's Lane
Children & dogs: Both welcome

The Walk

1. From the entrance to the **car park**, take the path that leads uphill behind the **toilet block**. Turn right onto the road around the bay. If the tide is out, take the steps down to the **beach** and walk along to the **harbour**. If not, continue along the road and take the ramps down onto the **promenade** instead.

2. Skirt around the harbour. At the harbour beach, take the road uphill between the **church** and **arches**. Turn left in front of the **boat trip sheds** towards the lifeboat stations. Pass the **old lifeboat station** and then the new one.

There has been a lifeboat station in Tenby since 1852. The first lifeboat, the Grace Darling, cost just £125, the equivalent of £12-15,000 today. All-weather lifeboats now cost £2.2 million and even the inshore lifeboats cost £89,000!

From here, the view encompasses most of Carmarthen Bay, all the way round to the Gower peninsula and Worm's Head island. As you continue around the headland, the view incorporates the old fort and Caldey Island.

Follow the path around the **headland** and up to the **castle** for the best views of the town and its surroundings. Take the steps down towards the town, turn left at the bottom of the steps and then right to pass under the **stone arch** which was once the castle gatehouse.

Tenby's famous medieval 'Five Arches'

The path returns to the harbour. At the corner with **St Julian's Street,** take **Bridge Street** with the harbour on your right. Pass the **blue plaque** commemorating George Eliot's visit to Tenby and then take a left into **Sergeant's Lane.**

The lane is lined with tables for those tasting Harbwr Brewery's craft beer, but for the main entrance to the pub, continue to the end of the lane and turn right. It's along the **High Street** on the right.

3. Continue along the High Street almost as far as the **church**. Turn left into **Church Street**, then right into **St George's Street** and through the **arch**.

This archway is known as Five Arches. Initially, it was one of only two gates into the medieval walled town. Visitors had to turn at right angles to enter, making it difficult to force entry with a battering ram. Over time, traffic flow became the priority over defence, so one entrance was turned into five.

Turn right and follow the **old town walls** along and then to the right. Turn left onto the road at the **seafront**. At the fork,

Colourful Georgian houses surround Tenby's Old Harbour

keep left past **Castle View house**. After about 400 metres, pass **Gas Lane** on the right – the road leading to the car park.

4. Take the next footpath on the right up some steps and under trees to join **Slippery Back**. Continue along this lane, which turns into a path and then back into a lane, for almost a kilometre to the **A478**.

5. Turn right along the road, and very shortly right again down a drive with a **'Waterwynch Estate' sign**, heading directly towards the sea. After about 600 metres, take the **footpath** on the right between a private drive and a farm gate.

6. At a junction of paths, continue ahead for a short detour down to a lovely sandy beach, which is well worth a visit but only accessible when the tide is not high. The route continues to the right, following the **acorn waymarker**. As this path continues uphill for some distance, there are several **benches** strategically placed for those who need a rest.

At the next junction of paths, turn left into **Allen's View**, *a garden with wooden sculptures and a picnic spot that was donated by Jessie Allen in 1965.*

At the end of the garden, turn left back onto the **coast path**.

7. At a tarmac lane by the **gate to Clovers and Kingfisher**, take the waymarked footpath downhill to the left of the lane. At the end of the lane, there is just a short distance to walk before reaching the ramp down to the **car park** on the right to complete the walk. ♦

Caldey Island

Caldey Island has been home to a community of monks on and off since the sixth century when the first monastery was built there. The island currently has around 40 residents plus the Cistercian monks. In the UK, the Crown owns the land between high and low tide, but on Caldey Island, Henry I gave the land away down to the low water mark, making this island very unusual in being entirely privately owned.

Brown's Hotel in Laugharne was the poet Dylan Thomas' favourite bar

Brown's Hotel
Laugharne

What to expect:
Tranquil views, sheltered sunken paths and a touch of Dylan Thomas

Distance/Time: 10.5 kilometres / 6½ miles. Allow 4 hours

Start: Car park near the castle at the junction of The Grist and The Strand. Free

Grid ref: SN 301 107

Ordnance Survey map: Explorer 177, *Carmarthen & Kidwelly*

The Pub: Brown's Hotel, King Street, Laugharne SA33 4RY | 01994 427688 | www.browns.wales

Walk outline: A figure-of-eight walk starting at Laugharne Castle. The first loop follows the estuary, taking in poet Dylan Thomas' writing shed and the Boathouse, where he lived. It continues along lovely shady lanes, lined with wildflowers, to the churchyard with Dylan Thomas' grave and back into town. The second loop heads west along more lanes, around a meadow and back along the coast path at the bottom of the cliff.

Brown's Hotel was Dylan Thomas' regular haunt - he famously gave the bar's 'phone number as his own. It is now owned by the Brown's boutique hotel chain. Drinkers are welcomed into the 'breakfast room', and diners into the restaurant.

'Dylan's Bar' at Brown's Hotel

▶ Brown's Hotel at a glance
Open: Mon-Sat 3.30pm-late. Sunday 12pm-late
Brewery/company: Freehouse
Ales and wine: Focus on red wine, gin, champagne and a few cocktails. Liqueur coffees popular with diners. Local Penderyn whisky
Food: By Dexters Steakhouse & Grill. Vegetarian and gluten-free options. Other dietary requirements catered for with notice. Restaurant open Mon-Sat 5.30-9pm, Sun 12-3pm & 6.30-9pm. Need to book
Accommodation: 14 boutique rooms
Outside: Small rear garden
Children & dogs: Children welcome. Dogs welcome in the breakfast room, bar and 11 of the hotel rooms

Dylan Thomas' Boat House overlooks the Taf Estuary

The Walk

1. From the **car park**, cross the **bridge** by the **ford** with the castle on your left and estuary on your right. Follow the path past the castle along the base of the cliffs. After about 300 metres, continue over the rocks ahead and up a **flight of steps** signposted 'Dylan Thomas Boat House'.

At the top of the steps, turn right onto the lane. Look out for the **garage** on your right, perched on the edge of the cliff, that Dylan Thomas used as his writing shed. A little further along, **Dylan Thomas' Boathouse** can be seen below.

When you reach a tarmac drive, head straight over through the woods, signposted 'Wales Coast Path'. To your right, the sandy shores of the estuary have now become salt marsh.

The path continues in the same direction across a couple of fields and passes a vegetable garden on the right.

2. Pass to the left of the **stone house** (shown on the map as Delacorse) and follow their drive for about 600 metres to a lane. Ignore signs for the Wales Coast Path as it turns right towards Brixtarw.

Turn left onto the lane and follow it

downhill to the right, past the entrance to **Delacorse Uchaf.** Look out for the kissing gate into the **cemetery** on the right and follow the path around the **church**, through a grove of yew trees and over the **footbridge** into the 'new' cemetery. Head uphill to the **white cross** that bears the names of both Dylan Thomas and his wife Caitlin.

3. Continue uphill to leave the cemetery and turn right onto the track.

Follow this track gently downhill to the **outskirts of the town**.

At the junction with the entrance to the **Dylan Coastal Resort** on the left, take the road downhill with houses on each side. Head straight over the junction where the road bends to the right, signposted 'Foreshore'. The **castle** can be seen directly ahead.

At **The Coach House**, turn right to the white **Town Hall** and right again onto the main road through the town. **Brown's Hotel** is a short distance along on the right.

4. From Brown's, retrace your steps back to the **Town Hall** and continue downhill past the castle entrance and public **toilets** on the left. At **The Grist**, opposite the car park where the walk started, head past the cross between the **Fountain Inn** and the **Cross House Inn.**

Panoramic views over the Taf Estuary from Laugharne Castle

Follow this quiet road up a wooded valley past **The Lacques water pump** and then following a **stream** on the left.

Take the left fork to pass in front of **Willow Glen** and then along the drive leading to **Skerry House**. When you reach the house, follow the narrow path between the house and the **stream**, over a stile and along another sunken path through **woodland**.

5. From walking in an enclosed valley, the path opens up into a delightful meadow that is grazed by cows over the winter months. A few metres ahead, turn diagonally right past the wooden pole holding power lines. Continue uphill, bending round to the left to keep another set of power lines above you and to your right.

Where this path meets a tractor track, continue in the same direction, this time downhill past a building to a road.

Turn right. Where this road bends to the right, turn left onto the dirt track. At the top of the track, there are views of the sea and Caldey Island, soon hidden as the track drops to the **A4066**.

6. At the junction with the road, head straight over down the hill. At the bottom of the slope, turn left over a cattle grid, following the **Wales Coast Path** sign.

This track continues for around 1.5 kilometres with the reclaimed marshes on the right and cliffs on the left.

Follow the Wales Coast Path through a gate uphill through the woods to the top of the cliff. As the path continues downhill and back to the town, there are views over the castle to the right. ♦

Laugharne Castle

The Normans had more ships than the Welsh, so they built a series of castles around the coast. This allowed them to push inland, and if the Welsh attacked, they could retreat to the castle and wait there for supplies and reinforcements. This approach was not too successful in Laugharne, as the castle was captured twice by the Welsh and finally by the Parliamentarians who dismantled it during the Civil War.

The comfortable modern bar at the Inn at the Sticks

Inn at the Sticks
Llansteffan

What to expect:
A gentle walk with easy climbs and far-reaching views. Paths can be slippery when wet

Distance/time: 7 kilometres / 4 miles. Allow 2½ hours

Start: Car park at the north end of Llansteffan Beach. Free at the time of writing. If full, use the car park at the south end of the beach

Grid ref: SN 355 108

Ordnance Survey map: Explorer 177, *Carmarthen & Kidwelly*

The Pub: Inn at the Sticks, High Street, Llansteffan SA33 5JG | 01267 241177 | www.innatthesticks.co.uk

Walk outline: A short walk into the centre of this pretty village quickly takes you to the pub. After that, the route passes the castle and progresses to St Anthony's Well. It then climbs to join the Wales Coast Path along the clifftops, with fantastic views. Return either along the beach or through the woods — known locally as 'The Sticks'.

The Inn at the Sticks is generally more sedate than the Castle Inn next door and is proud of the quality of its locally sourced food. It is a historic building, with Solomon's gravestone under the fireplace and a secret door leading to the adjoining building. If you want to know more, ask at the bar!

A welcome freehouse

▶ The Inn at the Sticks at a glance
Open: Wed-Sat 12-10pm, Sun 12-4pm. Sometimes longer hours in summer
Brewery/company: Freehouse
Ales and wine: Wine chosen to go well with menu. Fruit ciders and Welsh beers on tap
Food: Sourced within 10 miles wherever possible, all made in-house. Vegan and vegetarian options. Children's menu
Accommodation: Five rooms above the pub, three are dog-friendly
Outside: Beer garden behind the pub
Children & dogs: Both welcome in the pub and accommodation

The Walk

1. From the entrance to the **car park**, head straight inland on the pavement signposted 'Village'. At the far end of the field on the left, take the footpath diagonally left between gardens. Ignore the next path on the left, continuing gently uphill until you reach the **High Street** with houses in front of you. Turn left past the **village store** and towards the **church**.

2. The Inn at the Sticks is on the right, opposite the church.

With the inn at your back, walk ahead with the **church** to your right. You will soon see the castle ahead. Just after entering the **woods**, take the **right fork** up a concrete drive signposted 'Llansteffan Castle'.

A little further, turn left for a short detour into the **castle**.

Continue up the concrete drive past **Castlehill Cottage** on the left and follow the drive to the left when you can see a high estate wall ahead. Turn left at a sign to 'St Anthony's Cottage' and follow the valley down to the bay, taking a left fork at the **Bwthyn Sant Antwn sign** to avoid turning into their private drive.

3. Keep an eye out for the gate to **St Anthony's Well** on the right.

Legend has it that in the 6th century, a local hermit called Anthony used to baptize

converts to Christianity using water from this well. The water became renowned for having healing properties, so this modest well became a site of pilgrimage.

Once you have reached the bay, turn right through **two white gates** and follow the path to the right at **Y Ffesantri**. This path rises with St Anthony's Cottage garden wall on the right and a bank on the left. Pass through a farm gate with a National Trust sign into **Lord's Park farm**. Continue gently uphill on this grassy track through several gates until you pass the farm.

Continue along what is now a tarmac lane, round a right-hand bend. At the end of the field on the left, take the footpath left between hedges. You are now on the **Wales Coast Path**. This section of the path can be slippery when wet.

4. As the route bends to the left to follow the line of the cliffs, there are occasional views through gaps in the hedge. Just a little further along, the view opens up completely, with some well-placed benches to admire it from.

You can just see Laugharne on the far side of the estuary to the right — see walk 2. To

Llansteffan Castle guards the broad mouth of the River Towy

the left, you can see the multiple estuaries feeding into Carmarthen Bay, and the land directly in front of you, although distant, is the Gower Peninsula, with Worm's Head island jutting out of the sea to its right. In the very far distance, on a clear day, you can just see the Devon coast.

Follow the path through this '**Celtic Rainforest**', around the headland and down past a **stone cottage** on your left — Y Ffesantri. Return through the two white gates flanking St Anthony's Cottage, glancing left from the bridge to admire the garden sculptures.

5. This is **Scott's Bay**. If the tide is out, you can return to the car park along the beach. Please take care, as the cliffs are steep — if you are at all unsure about whether you will get round before the tide cuts you off, then stay on the path.

If you are not taking the beach route, choose the path directly ahead that rises partway up the cliffs, signposted 'Wales Coast Path'. The route passes through woodland for about 0.75 kilometres.

These woods are known as The Sticks. There used to be a stage near the artistic metal bench where they held the Mock-Mayor Making Ceremony and other events.

Just after the **commemorative metal bench**, take the left fork back to the lane leading into the village. After about 200 metres, at the information board for **The Croft**, turn right downhill towards the car park and river. Cross the car park and turn left onto the coast path.

If you choose to walk back along the beach, look for the children's playground for the entrance to this car park.

Follow the path for a short distance to the walk's starting point to complete the walk. ♦

Celtic Rainforest

The ancient woodland at Wharley Point is officially 'coastal slope woodland', but is also known as 'Celtic rainforest' because it is such a complex and biodiverse ecosystem. Its proximity to the sea means that temperatures are higher than inland, the habitat has additional light reflected from the water, and rainfall is lower than inland. Of particular note, Wharley Point is home to maidenhair ferns, sea spleenwort and a couple of centipedes rare in Wales.

The creeper covered Kings Head Inn at Llangennith

Kings Head Inn
Llangennith

What to expect:
Good paths through town and over hilly ground with grand views

Distance/time: 12 kilometres / 7½ miles. Allow 3-3½ hours. (Alternative shorter route without loop from Rhossili, 9 kilometres/ 5½ miles.)

Start: National Trust car park at Rhossili (charge). Parking is also available at Hillend (charge) and there is a limited amount of on-street parking near the King's Head Inn

Grid ref: SS 415880

Ordnance Survey map: Explorer 164, *Gower*

The Pub: Kings Head Inn, Llangennith, Gower SA3 1HX | 01792 386212 | www.kingsheadgower.co.uk

Walk outline: Rhossili Bay is one of the best-loved beaches in the UK. Three miles of golden sand form a crescent that faces the open sea and the setting sun. This walk makes the most of the views, rising to the highest point of Rhossili Down on the way to the pub and dropping to the coast path on the return leg. A loop around the peninsula allows a closer view of Worm's Head, glimpses of the cliffs of the south Gower coast and a field of sunflowers in summer.

The Kings Head is housed in three 17th Century stone buildings right in the heart of Llangennith village. The south-facing patio garden has views over the medieval church with its recently restored carved oak lychgate.

Kings Head metal sign

▶ The Kings Head Inn at a glance

Open: Daily from 11am-11pm, 12-10.30pm on Sunday

Brewery/company: Freehouse

Ales and wine: Welsh real ales. Extensive range of malt whiskies from Scotland (as well as the Welsh Penderyn) and gins

Food: Home-made food 11am-9pm, booking recommended. Favourites include home cooked curries and pizza, plus traditional pub food

Accommodation: The modern rooms are in three buildings adjacent to the pub. Underfloor heating and 28"TV. Surf board storage available

Outside: South-facing patio with benches in front of the pub

Children & dogs: Child-friendly; one bar welcomes well-behaved pets

The Walk

1. From the **car park** at **Rhossili**, return to the **village** and follow the waymarked **Wales Coast Path** to the left of the church then left down the track. From here, the route is visible rising steeply up the hill ahead.

Pass a house on the right and head uphill before the garage. Where the footpath bends to the right, look for an opening in the gorse directly uphill and take that instead. Continue uphill to the **trig point**.

The views from here encompass Carmarthen Bay to the north, the Gower Peninsula to the east, Devon across the Bristol Channel to the south and Rhossili Bay and Worm's Head to the south west.

Keep an eye out for the blowhole on the north side of Worm's Head. When the tide is high and the conditions are right, it spurts a fountain of water into the air as high as the island itself.

From the trig point, continue to head north with the sea

to your left until the path descends from the ridge. Fork right twice. At a clear junction, take the long zig-zags right and then left down to **Sweyne's Howes** – a pair of neolithic burial chambers.

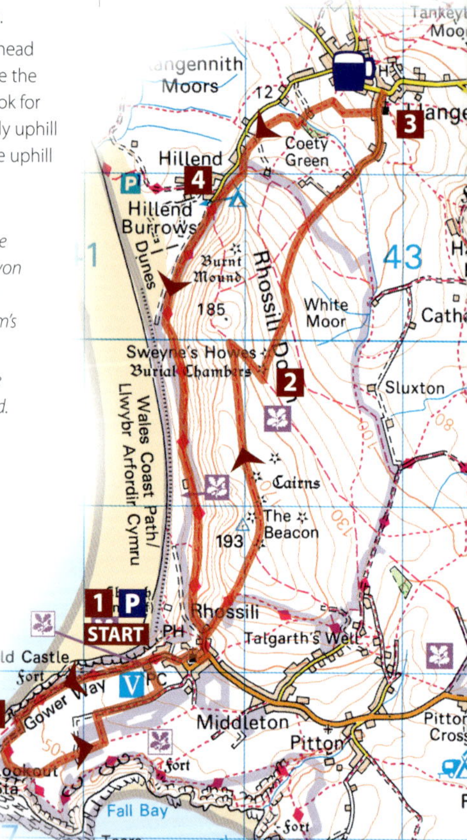

0   1 km
½ mile

Overlooking Worms Head from the top of Rhossili Down

2. With the northern burial chamber slightly above the path and to your left, head northeast.

At a waymarker, fork right (straight ahead) towards the village. At a five-way junction of paths, head directly downhill on the bridlepath, which turns into a track and then a minor road. Follow this road into the village and to the **pub**.

3. From the pub, head back down the road opposite with the **church** on the left. Just past the farm entrance on the left, take the public footpath between houses on the right, towards the **sand dunes and sea**.

Pass through a gate into a field. Keep the hedge on your right and continue through another gate hidden in the corner. Continue with the hedge now on your left to another gate, then downhill towards the base of **Rhossili Down** and the sea.

Follow the clearly signed path around the house at the bottom of this field and continue downhill to a **stream**. Turn left and cross at the **bridge**. The path heads up the hill. Follow it for around 20 metres then take the gate on the right into a field, directly towards the sand dunes.

Look for and cross the **stone stile**

Rhossili beach is often voted one of the most beautiful in Wales

diagonally opposite, follow the path through another gate and then head directly across the middle of the next field.

Cross the track and continue in the same direction with the hedge on your left.

At the end of the field, follow the path steeply uphill, then turn right on a gentle descent to the **holiday park**.

There are clear views of Worm's Head from this path – another great opportunity to see the blow hole in action. On a clear day, Lundy Island is also visible in the distance.

4. Just before the holiday park, turn left and follow the **Wales Coast Path** between Rhossili Down and the beach. If the tide is out, it is possible to walk along the beach instead.

Towards the end of the bay, the path ascends into **Rhossili village**.

Retrace your steps towards the church and turn right on the path immediately before it. At the end of the path, continue along the road back to the car park.

Take the track between the **Worm's Head Hotel** and the **car park,** past the **toilets** and along the peninsula.

5. Where the track U-turns to the left, follow the path diagonally to the left, signposted Wales Coast Path. The **Coastguard station** remains a distance off to the right. When the path reaches a drystone wall, follow this to the left.

Where the Wales Coast Path turns right to follow the cliffs, take the gate directly ahead to walk back along the middle of the peninsula, following the clear track as it bends left and then right through this medieval field system. Turn left off the track back to the car park. ♦

Gower flower power

Visitors have been enjoying sunflowers in Rhossili since 2018 when the National Trust reinstated the old medieval field strip system on land known as The Vile. They have chosen crops that are good for pollinators and provide seeds for birds later in the year. If you want to see the sunflowers in bloom, visit towards the end of the summer. During this period, the National Trust car park is likely to be congested, so consider parking at Hillend instead.

The cosy traditional bar at the King Arthur Hotel

King Arthur Hotel
Reynoldston

What to expect:
Visit to Arthur's Stone burial chamber and stunning views. Boggy in places

Distance/Time: 7.75 kilometres / 4¾ miles. Allow 2¾ hours

Start: King Arthur Hotel or Llanrhidian (point 3) – some on-road parking in both places

Grid ref: SS 482 899 or SS 498 920

Ordnance Survey map: Explorer 164, *Gower*

The Pub: King Arthur Hotel, Reynoldston, Swansea SA3 1AD
01792 390775 | www.kingarthurhotel.co.uk

Walk outline: From the hotel, there is a short, sharp climb onto the Cefn Bryn ridge. The reward is a fine, uninterrupted view across most of the peninsula. The ground on the north side of the ridge tends to be a little boggy, so boots are recommended for the drop down to Oldwalls and Llanrhidian. After climbing back onto the ridge, take a moment to enjoy Arthur's Stone burial chamber before the short journey back to Reynoldston.

The King Arthur Hotel is named after Arthur's Stone and boasts a sword in reception. Could it possibly be Excalibur itself? With a focus on locally-sourced food and beer, a cosy log fire in the bar and plenty of garden space, this is a deservedly popular pub.

Legendary hotel

▶ King Arthur Hotel at a glance

Open: Daily from 10am-11pm

Brewery/company: Family-owned freehouse

Ales and wine: Locally-sourced beer including Gower Gold and Double Dragon. Extensive wine list

Food: Bar menu plus restaurant-style specials, catering to different diets. Locally sourced. Breakfast 10-11 am, lunch and dinner 12-9 pm

Accommodation: 19 B&B rooms, 4 self-catering cottage apartments

Outside: Large garden in front of pub. Glass veranda shelters a few tables

Children & dogs: Children are welcome. Dogs in garden only

The Walk

1. From the **hotel**, head diagonally left across the **green** to the corner of a garden wall. Turn left onto the road, then in a few metres, turn right opposite the **Post Office** to ascend the ridge. The path is well-used, but in places, it is narrow with gorse bushes on each side.

The view from the ridge extends north over the Loughor estuary, west to Rhossili Down and the open sea beyond, and south across the Bristol Channel to Devon and Lundy.

Continue straight over two paths that cross this one until the path bends gently to the right and you are gradually heading downhill across the slope. Loughor estuary is now below to your left and the ridge above to your right. Turn left where paths cross and the path ahead

narrows distinctly. Fork right after about 40 metres, towards the gorse bushes, downhill. Keep the gorse mainly to your left, then follow the peaty path for some distance downhill towards **Oldwalls village**. As you enter the trees, a gate becomes visible to the right.

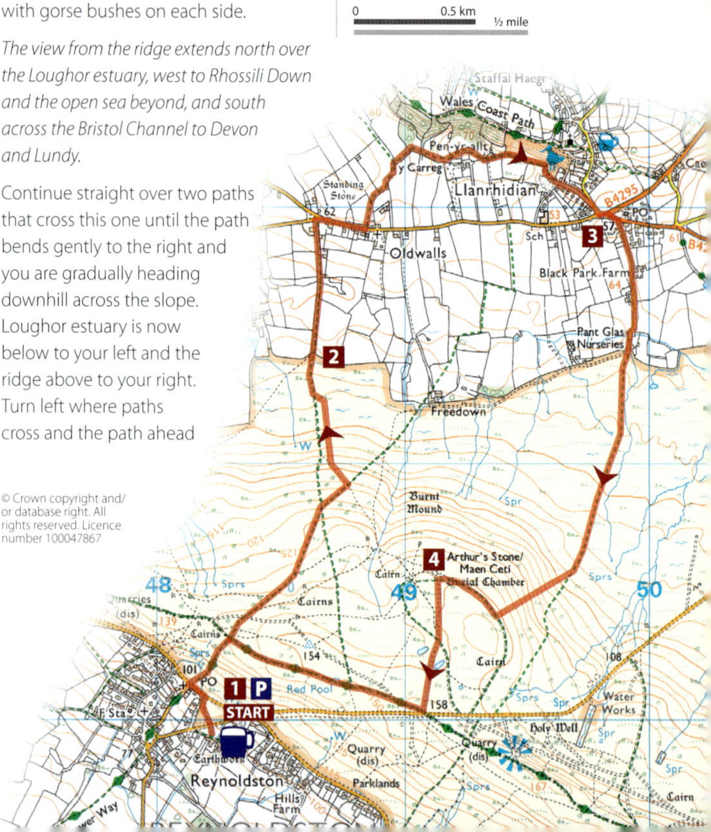

There are panoramic views from the Cefn Bryn ridge

2. Through the gate, follow the track between hedges to **Oldwalls**. The route follows the main road to the right for about 175 metres. There are no pavements — beware of traffic.

Turn left down the side of the house with a **red post box** on its front wall. Cross the field to the **stone stile** just about visible in the hedge ahead. Cross the stile and follow the fence on the left until it turns a corner, then cross the field ahead and turn left along the nearside of the hedge. Keep the hedge on your right as you pass through two gates and the path bends to the right.

Go through another gate and up a rise towards a house. Follow the signs for the **permissive footpath** around a couple of houses, and then the waymarked route to and through the **farm** at **Pen-yr-Allt**.

Views to the left now include the salt marshes flanking the Loughor estuary. These are in the intertidal zone, completely covered for a few hours each day around high tide. The lamb reared on these marshes has a distinctly salty flavour.

The waymarked path continues alongside the **farmhouse garden** and the top of a steep slope down to the left until it reaches **Llanrhidian**. On arriving

Evening light illuminates Arthur's Stone Neolithic burial chamber

at the village, walk straight ahead on **Malt Hall** and turn right at the end of the road onto **Mill Lane**.

3. Carefully cross the **B4295** and turn onto the **B4271** to the right of the **petrol station**. Almost opposite the entrance to the petrol station, take the small unnamed lane on the right.

Cefn Bryn soon appears ahead, forming a long ridge on the skyline.

After around 450 metres on this lane, the tarmac ends and it turns right, away from a farm and beneath power lines. Leave the lane here to continue up the footpath ahead.

Just after crossing the power lines, turn left through a kissing gate, then follow the path across **moorland** onto the **ridge**. Close to the bottom of the moor, ignore the path to the left that crosses a **ford**. Although the path fractures around boggy bits and re-joins itself, the overall route is clear. Aim for the bulge of the ridge right of centre.

Near the top, this path meets a grassy ride running along the hill. Turn right on this path to **Arthur's Stone burial chamber**.

4. Follow the path around to the left in front of Arthur's stone and to the car park

on the skyline ahead. At the **car park**, stay on this side of the road and take the **bridleway** to the right that leads diagonally away from the road.

After about 50 metres, fork left, past **Red Pool** on the right. At a crossroads of paths in a slight dip (before reaching the solitary wooden pole), turn left and retrace your steps down the path into **Reynoldston**. ◆

Cefn Bryn – 'Backbone of Gower'

Over centuries, Cefn Bryn common land has been grazed by sheep, cattle and ponies, resulting in a wildlife habitat of international importance. It may seem bleak to us, but provides a home to skylarks, the threatened marsh fritillary butterfly and the well-camouflaged brown hare. In spring, the northern slopes have swathes of cottongrass bobbing in the breeze. The ponies can be very friendly – don't be surprised if they sidle up and give you a nudge!

The family-friendly Woodman pub at Black Pill

What to expect:
Formal garden, wooded valley, short section of beach. Hilly, good paths and tracks

The Woodman
Black Pill, Swansea

Distance/time: 8 kilometres / 5 miles. Allow 3 hours

Start: Woodman pub – public parking next to pub car park

Grid ref: SS 618 905

Ordnance Survey map: Explorer 164, *Gower*

The Pub: The Woodman, Mumbles Road, Blackpill, Swansea SA3 5AS | 01792 402700 | www.chefandbrewer.com/pubs/west-glamorgan/woodman

Walk outline: Trees and shrubs feature strongly on this walk, first in Clyne Gardens and then through the wooded Clyne Valley Country Park. Clyne Gardens belonged to a plant-hunter and sport a wide variety of interesting specimens, including famed collections of rhododendrons and azaleas. A steep walk to the top of the gardens is rewarded with an impressive view over Swansea Bay.

The Woodman is a popular pub-restaurant that prides itself on being dog-friendly, with water, biscuits, ice cream and even sausages for our furry friends. Close to the coast path and at the entrance to Clyne Gardens, it is the perfect place to grab refreshments. Booking recommended.

Doggy treats

▶ The Woodman at a glance

Open: 11am-11pm Mon-Fri. 9.30am-11pm Sat. 9.30am-10.30pm Sun
Brewery/company: Greene King
Ales and wine: Impressive wine list, cask ales and gin selection
Food: Classic pub food, complemented by weekly chef's specials. Vegetarian and vegan options. Roasts on Sundays. Kitchen open from 11.30 am to 9 pm Mon-Fri, 9.30 am to 9 pm Sat & Sun
Accommodation: None
Outside: Beer garden with tables and sun shades
Children & dogs: Both welcome

The Walk

1. From the **car park**, turn right up the lane into **Clyne Gardens**. Pass **Clyne Lodge** on your right, continue straight up the tarmac drive and take a left turn signposted 'Bog Garden' just before the **toilets** on the right.

To shorten the walk by about 2 kilometres, or if you have no interest in the gardens, continue straight past the toilets to Clyne Castle (point 3).

Keep the stream on your left until you reach **Admiral's Tower.** Bear left, cross the **stream** and continue uphill with the stream now on your right. At a junction of paths, turn right and continue uphill past an entrance to the park with a **gatehouse**.

Stay on the **tarmac drive** as it bends to the right, then bear left on a **narrower tarmac path** that heads slightly uphill for a few metres before dropping.

At the signpost turn right towards **Joy Cottage**, over the red and white **Japanese bridge**. On the far side of the bridge, keep left up the **formal steps** then continue uphill to the right. Follow the edge of the **open parkland** to your left and **wooded valley** to your right.

Huge specimen trees frame Clyne Castle

2. At a junction of paths, take the second left, keeping the parkland to your left and trees to your right. Follow this path as it turns into a dirt track through the trees and bear left to cross the open **grassy slope.**

This is a perfect spot to take a break, admire the view over Swansea Bay and have a picnic.

On the far side of the grassy slope, turn right onto a path that meanders down the hill.

Look out for the huge **Giant Redwood** and **Monterey Cypresses** in front of **Clyne Castle** to your left.

Cross the narrow **stone bridge** and turn left in front of the castle to join **Mill Lane**.

3. Turn left along the lane. Turn into the **small car park** on the right, opposite the more modern part of the **Clyne Castle development**. Take the stony track on the left signposted **'Keeper's Path'**, uphill into the woods. A little way up, there is a round **stone tower** on the right.

Stay on this track for around 1 kilometre, ignoring side paths, until a field on the left.

Sunlight and dappled shade beneath the trees in Clyne Gardens

4. At the end of the field, turn left along the **bridleway**. Keep on the right-hand path, as the left-hand one is designated for cyclists only. The path bends right away from the field boundary and heads gently downhill. Pass the **bike jumps course** on the right.

Continue heading straight downhill. The path becomes sunken. Shortly after a slightly muddy stretch, fork right, following the **blue waymarker.**

At a crossing of paths, turn left down the slope to join the tarmacked **Clyne Valley Trail.**

5. Turn left onto the trail for a short period. At the black signpost, turn right towards **Old Brick Works**. At the next junction, turn right. Take the right fork, then left towards 'Olchfa Lane'.

Follow this raised path for a few hundred metres. At the T-junction, turn right onto **Olchfa Lane**.

6. Where the path joins a tarmacked drive, continue straight on, cross a stream and then turn right towards **Black Pill**. At a fork with a gravel track, stay right on the tarmac. Pass a gate across the track, heading downhill to a grassy area.

Turn right towards Black Pill, and at the stream turn left. At the **wooden bridge**, cross the stream and turn left onto the old railway, now a **cycle path**.

7. At the end of the cycle path, cross the **'A' road** and head left and then right over a **footbridge** to join the **coast path**, with the bay on your left and Mumbles Pier visible ahead.

Just before the **filling station**, turn right back to the **'A' road** and the **Woodman pub** to complete the walk. ◆

Clyne Valley Country Park

Although the country park is now an idyllic mix of woodland and water features, it was once a hive of industry. This started in the 14th century with coal mining, which later attracted an ironworks and chemical works. Brickmaking thrived in the valley well into the last century. All this activity needed transport, starting with a tramway that became the London Midland Scottish Railway. The Clyne Valley Cycleway follows the old railway line today.

Open fire and local memorabilia at the Prince of Wales Inn

Prince of Wales Inn
Kenfig

What to expect:
Dunes, a lake, birdsong and wildflowers. Slow in soft sand, some muddy patches

Distance/time: 6.5 kilometres / 4 miles. Allow 2½ hours.

Start: Kenfig Reserve Centre—with parking (free at the time of writing) and toilets

Grid ref: SS 801 810

Ordnance Survey map: Explorer 151, *Cardiff & Bridgend*

The Pub: Prince of Wales Inn, Kenfig, Bridgend CF33 4PR

01656 740356 | www.princeofwalesinn.co.uk

Walk outline: A varied walk through a nationally important dune complex. Starting at the visitor centre, the route skirts Kenfig Pool and woodland before heading through dunes to the coast. After a section on the coast path, the route swings inland following clear waymarkers through dunes, machair, boggy areas and broadleaf woodland, ending at the pub. The return leg follows the shore of Kenfig Pool

The 15th century Prince of Wales Inn is thought by some to be one of the most haunted pubs in Wales, possibly because of its history. It has served as the town hall, a courtroom, dance hall, Sunday school room and a mortuary for shipwrecked sailors.

Painted inn sign

▶ The Prince of Wales Inn at a glance

Open: Mondays 4-11 pm, Tuesday to Sunday 12 noon-11 pm
Brewery/company: Freehouse
Ales and wine: Bass beer and local ales served directly from the cask
Food: Traditional Welsh dishes as well as more usual pub favourites. Home-made with locally sourced ingredients where possible
Accommodation: None
Outside: Beer garden and marquee
Children & dogs: One dog-friendly room. Children welcome

The Walk

1. Take the path to the right of the **visitor centre** towards the Wales Coast Path. After a few metres, at a junction of paths, turn right, signposted 'Wales Coast Path and Kenfig Pool'. From a grassy area, head for the beach.

Covering 28 hectares (70 acres), Kenfig Pool is the largest natural lake in South Wales and attracts migratory birds in winter.

Continue along the path with **Kenfig Pool** on your right. At the fork, take a short diversion to the right to spend time in the **bird hide** overlooking the pool. Otherwise, fork left diagonally away from the pool.

2. Follow this path through the scrub with larger broadleaf trees 10-20 metres to your right.

You are now heading towards the sea; stay on the same rough bearing (west) to reach the **coast path**. If you are unsure which path to take, head for the sound of the waves.

Shortly after the trees thin, take the right fork. At crossing paths, head straight over to avoid climbing up dunes to the left. After another 60 metres or so, bear left around the edge of the boggy area and continue straight, out of the far end, over **dunes** to the **coast path**.

3. Turn right and follow the coast path for about 1 kilometre.

4. Turn right at the waymarkers, a short distance before a **fenced area of dunes**. Follow these waymarkers in an easterly direction all the way across the dunes back to the **road** – around 2 kilometres. At a crossing of waymarked paths close to the road, choose the path straight ahead, to meet the road close to the **pub**.

A path crosses the dunes close to Kenfig Pool

5. Continue along the road past the pub. Pass **Kenfig Farm** and **The Barns** on the left. Before the next house on the left (**Cotswold House**), turn right at the Footpath sign, towards **Kenfig Pool**. Pass through two vehicle gates opposite each other and then a pedestrian gate between the building on the left and shed on the right. There is now an uninterrupted view of the pool ahead.

6. Head diagonally right across the meadow to the corner of the hedge, then follow the boundary down to the lake. Turn left at the water and follow the path along the shore, over several stiles, back to the beach at the start of the walk.

7. Turn left and retrace your steps back to the visitor centre to compete the walk. ♦

Kenfig – the shifting sands of time

In 1140, Anglo-Normans established Kenfig in Welsh territory. The locals were not happy about this invasion and repeatedly attacked the town. The people of Kenfig survived these attacks, but could not survive the shifting sands. Ultimately, the town was buried, and only scant remains of the castle are visible today. Peace has returned to the area and the dunes provide an internationally significant habitat for endangered species.

The Old Swan Inn sits at the heart of pretty Llantwit Major

Old Swan Inn
Llantwit Major

What to expect:
Interesting walk through historic town; farmland to coast

Distance/Time: : 4.75 kilometres / 3 miles. Allow 1¾ hours

Start: Public car park next to Town Hall, opposite the Old Swan Inn. If full, alternative car park at beach, at point 4

Grid ref: SS 967 687

Ordnance Survey map: Explorer 151, *Cardiff & Bridgend*

The Pub: The Old Swan, Church St, Llantwit Major CF61 1SB. 01446 792230 | www.knifeandforkfood.co.uk/venue/the-old-swan-inn/

Walk outline: This varied walk starts in the historic town of Llantwit Major, visiting St Illtud's church before crossing pasture and arable farmland to reach the coast path. The route continues along the distinctive Blue Lias limestone clifftops before dropping to the rocky beach, café and car park. The route returns to the village along a shallow valley, via an impressive medieval stone dovecot.

The Old Swan Inn is in the centre of the village, opposite the Town Hall and next to the medieval town square. It's a 16th-century building that housed a mint during the Civil War and, rumour has it, was once the centre of the local smuggling trade. The pub holds a beer festival in the garden three times a year.

Sunny beer garden

▶ The Old Swan Inn at a glance

Open: Mon-Sat 12-11pm, Sunday 12-10.30pm
Brewery/company: Freehouse
Ales and wine: A variety of local ales and Welsh whisky. Decent selection of gin
Food: Classic pub food with more ambitious alternatives. Vegetarian and vegan options
Accommodation: None
Outside: Beer garden with benches and sunshades
Children & dogs: Children welcome. Dogs in the bar area only

Medieval monastic dovecot

The Walk

1. Leaving the **car park**, turn left between the **Town Hall** and the **Old Swan Inn**. Pass the **Town Square** on the right. At **St Illtud's Church**, head into the **churchyard** and down the left side of the church.

Enter through the modern glass doors to see the Celtic crosses in the Galilee Chapel exhibition and early effigies within the church itself.

Exit the churchyard at the far side, cross the **stream** and turn left onto **Church Lane**. Where the lane bears left at **Chantry House**, take the **steps** to the right up the side of the house. At the top of the steps, dogleg right then left down the far side of the **Old Police Station**.

At the end of the drive, continue past the gates to the **Old Vicarage** onto a footpath between hedges. Leave the path after around 150 metres, where it turns to the left. Instead, climb the first of a series of **stone stiles** ahead.

Follow the edge of two fields, with the hedge on your left.

Cross to the far right-hand corner of the next field, *taking a moment to look up and enjoy the views over the Bristol Channel to the Devon coast in the distance.*

The hedge is now immediately on your right for one field. At the next field boundary, look ahead and to the left to spot the next **stone stile**. One more short section along a hedge and one more stile take you to another large field.

2. The line of the footpath runs straight across the field and down the right-hand side of the **copse** about 400 metres ahead. At the far end of the copse, head across another arable field towards the ruin (**Sheeplays Barn**).

When you reach the hedge, turn left to gently descend towards the sea. At the corner of the field, cross one more **stone stile**, head down some **stone steps** and towards the coast.

3. On reaching the well-defined **Wales Coast Path**, turn left. At a junction of paths, take the steps down to the **café**, **toilets** and rocky beach.

The distinctive cliffs here are made from limestone, and the beach is well-known for its fossils. Be warned—the cliffs are not stable. Please do any fossil-hunting away from the base of the cliffs, while also keeping an eye on the tides.

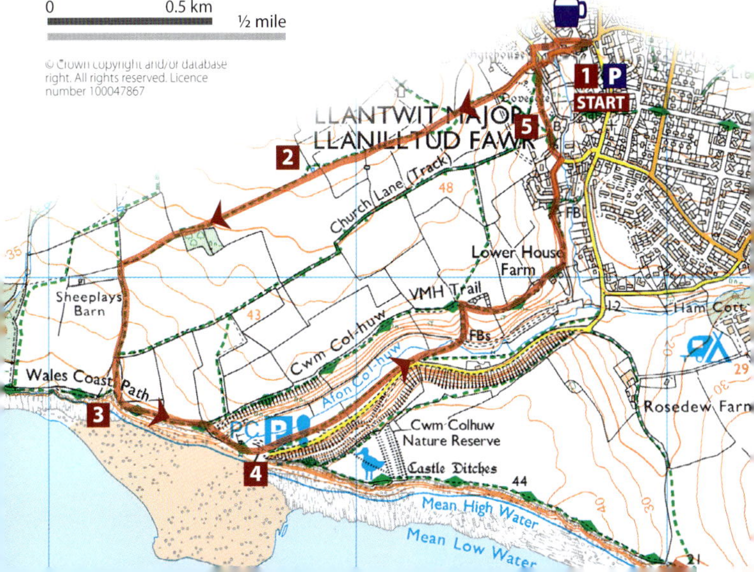

Dramatic stratified limestone cliffs dominate the coast at Llantwit Major

4. Cross the **stream** then turn left to follow it up a **wide valley**. When the path reaches a gate to the road, turn left through another gate and head diagonally left across the field past a **ford** and through a gap in bushes. Turn left almost immediately over the **footbridge**.

Follow the waymarker, climbing straight up the side of the valley to a stone track. Turn right to follow the track back into the village. It passes through **Lower House Farm** and then bears left, with the village now on the right.

Continue straight along the lane (**Flanders Road**), passing **Bramble** Cottage on the right. A little further along, ascend the drive immediately past **Flanders Farm** on the left, keeping **Flanders Barn** on your right. At the end of the barn, climb some **steps** and follow a wall on your right into a field containing a **stone dovecot**.

This is a fine example of a medieval dovecot, built in the 13th century to house birds for the monastery's table. Sadly, there is no sign of the tithe barn that used to stand immediately to its north.

5. Exit the field via the final **stone stile** of the walk, in front of a **row of cottages**. Turn left along the gravel drive, then right down the steps at the end of the row. You ascended the same steps early in the walk.

At the road, head straight ahead past **Chantry House** on your right and over the **stream**. At the end of the **churchyard** on your left, continue straight ahead on **Burial Lane** until you reach the Old Swan and the car park to complete the walk. ◆

Early seat of learning

In the 6th century, Llantwit Major became the first significant seat of learning in Britain when St Illtud founded a monastery here. Students included St Patrick and St David, the patron saints of Ireland and Wales, and Celtic Christianity spread from its teachings. The crosses in the Galilee Chapel are from the 9th to 11th centuries and are considered to be nationally important as rare artefacts of the early Celtic church.

The city-centre Tiny Rebel pub is owned by a local, award-winning brewery

Tiny Rebel
Cardiff

What to expect:
Green spaces and heritage buildings in an urban setting. Flat, mainly pavement

Distance/time: 7.5 kilometres/ 4½ miles. Allow 2-2½ hours

Start: Cardiff Central railway station

Grid ref: ST 182 758

Ordnance Survey map: Explorer 151, *Cardiff & Bridgend*

The Pub: Tiny Rebel, 25 Westgate St, Cardiff CF10 1DD | www.tinyrebel.co.uk/bars/cardiff

Walk outline: This walk makes the most of Cardiff's green infrastructure while exploring the key sights of Wales' capital city. Follow a broad tree-lined avenue from the city centre to the iconic Millennium Centre and Cardiff Bay waterfront. Continue through the Cardiff Bay Wetlands Reserve before returning along the banks of the Taff, passing the Principality Stadium and Cardiff Castle.

The Tiny Rebel is owned by the award-winning and vibrant Newport-based brewery of the same name. It is a quirky modern pub in a historic red brick building in the city centre, close to all the action on match days.

Varieties of beer mural

▶ The Tiny Rebel at a glance

Open: Daily 12pm-2am

Brewery/company: Tiny Rebel

Ales and wine: Craft beer from their own brewery and further afield.

Food: Menu is largely burger-based, including vegan options. Roasts on Sundays. Kitchen open 12-9 pm Mon-Sat, 12-6pm Sun

Accommodation: None

Outside: No outside space

Children & dogs: Dogs allowed, children welcome until 9pm

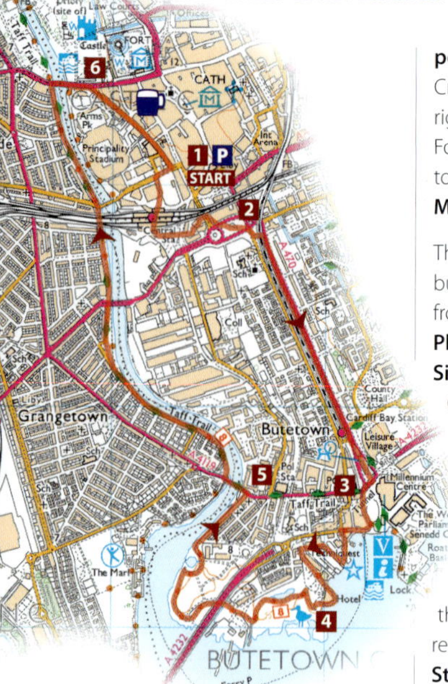

The Walk

1. Leave the **station** by the Penarth Road exit. Turn left along the side of the **car park**, right onto **Penarth Road** and first left onto **West Canal Wharf**. Where the road bends to the left, continue straight ahead between two buildings past a brightly coloured **sculpture**. With the roundabout to your right, cross two roads and enter **Callaghan Square**.

2. Walk between the **water feature** and the **statue of the Marquis of Bute** to the far corner of the square. Walk about 50m down **Bute Street**, then take the

pedestrian archway under the railway. Cross **Lloyd George Avenue** and turn right along the broad **avenue of trees**. Follow this route for about 1 kilometre to the distinctive copper-coloured **Millennium Centre**.

The avenue is set back from the road, but if you would like to walk further from the traffic, turn left into **Magretion Place** and then right down the length of **Silurian Park** before returning to **Lloyd George Avenue**.

3. Keeping the Millennium Centre on your left, head towards the redbrick **Pierhead building** and the waterfront.

Turn right along the front and follow the line of the bay past cafes and restaurants, three **docks** and the striking **St David's Hotel**.

4. Follow the brick path beside the **Cardiff Bay Wetlands Reserve**, then turn left on the path through the reserve.

At the stone **sculpture**, take a detour along the **boardwalk** to a platform that gives great views over the **lagoon**.

From the boardwalk, continue through the reserve, cross over the **mini roundabout** and under the road bridge into **Hamadryad Park**. Take the first path on the right to cross the park, then continue with the **River Taff** on your left until you reach **Clarence Road**.

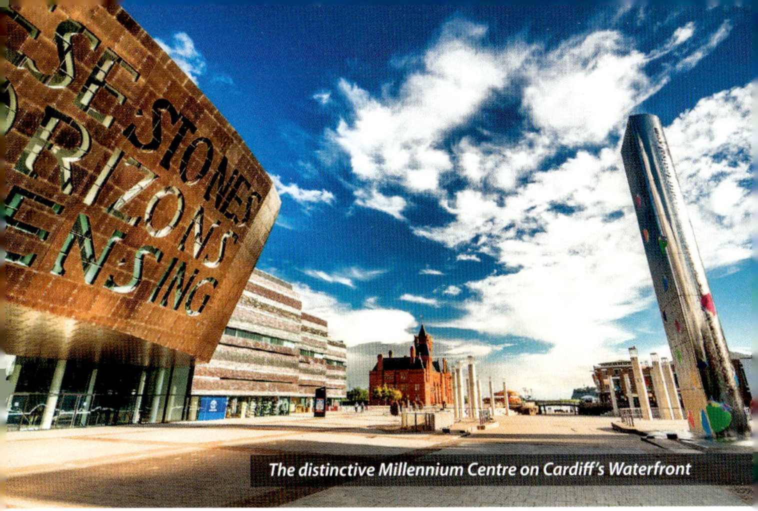

The distinctive Millennium Centre on Cardiff's Waterfront

5. Cross the **bridge** over the river, then cross the road to follow the **Taff Trail**, with the river now on your right. After around a kilometre, at the junction with **Llanbradach Street**, take the path to the right to continue following the river. Immediately after the **Principality Stadium**, home to Welsh Rugby Union, cross the river at **Cardiff Bridge**.

6. Take the first right (before the castle) into **Westgate Street**. The **Tiny Rebel** is about 150 metres down on the left, on the corner with **Quay Street**. From the pub, continue down **Westgate Street.** At the end of the road, dogleg right and then left past the **BBC Wales building** back to the station to complete the walk. ♦

Cardiff Bay Wetlands Reserve

The creation of the 500-acre Cardiff Bay lagoon in 1999 controversially destroyed large areas of wildlife-rich mudflats. In response, this small reserve was created to increase the wildlife value of the newly formed freshwater lake. Among other birds, watch out for great crested grebes bobbing up to the surface after diving for food. Information boards around the site will help you identify the wildlife.

The community-owned Waterloo Inn

Waterloo Inn
Nash village

What to expect:
Easy, mostly flat walk through nature reserve. No dogs allowed in reserve

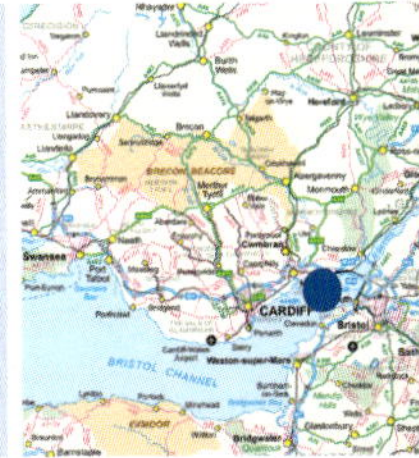

Distance/time: 7.25 kilometres / 4½ miles. Allow 2½ hours

Start: Newport Wetlands NNR car park (Fee, gates open 9 am-5 pm). There is also space to park near the pub at point 5

Grid ref: ST 334 834

Ordnance Survey map: Explorer 152, *Newport & Pontypool*

The Pub: Waterloo Inn, St Mary's Road, Nash NP18 2BZ | 01633 275429 | www.waterlooinnnash.wix.com/waterloo

Walk outline: The route dives straight into the Newport Wetlands nature reserve (free entry) and through reed beds where you are likely to spot warblers and perhaps even a glimpse of a bearded tit or resident otter. On joining the coast path, the route passes East Usk Lighthouse before following a lane inland and then crossing low-lying meadows to the village of Nash and its pub, before returning to the reserve.

The Waterloo Inn is a community-owned pub that has a café vibe in the restaurant, including a counter full of cakes and jars of sweets, and an old-fashioned pub vibe, complete with a dartboard and billiards table, in the bar.

Cake and sweet counter

▶ The Waterloo Inn at a glance

Open: Daily from 12 pm
Brewery/company: Harveys
Ales and wine: Welsh ale, fruit ciders. A good range of gin, whisky & rum
Food: Home-made pub grub. Vegan and vegetarian menus. Children's menu. Served until 8 pm
Accommodation: None, but the pub features in *Brit Stops*—campervans are welcome for a one-night stay if they drink in the pub
Outside: Small beer garden and children's play area
Children & dogs: Very child-friendly, with sweets, cakes and play area. Dogs in the bar

The Walk

1. From the **car park**, enter the **Newport Wetlands nature reserve**.

(Most of the reserve is not open to dogs. If you have a dog with you, instead of entering the reserve from the car park, turn right at the entrance and follow the Wales Coast Path signs around the outside of the reserve, to re-join the route at the lighthouse. This will add approximately 2 kilometres to the walk.)

Turn right towards and then past the **Newport Wetlands visitor centre**.

The visitor centre is well worth a visit to find out what wildlife has been spotted on site recently and indulge in a fantastic slice of cake and cup of tea overlooking one of their pools.

Continue on this gravel track until a crossing of paths at the top of a small rise.

2. Turn right, following a signpost to 'Orchid Trail and Sculpture Trail'. The power station is now visible ahead.

Stay on the path as it bears left, ignoring the smaller path ahead. At a T-junction, turn left under **electricity lines**.

Fencing has been erected on either side of this path to act as a bird hide. Allow plenty of time to gaze through the gaps in the fences, waiting for the wildlife to appear, or to simply enjoy the view over the pools.

At the next junction, dogleg left then right to continue in the same direction. Pylons are visible to the right, and the lighthouse to the left. The path passes through another **hide**, then the sea comes into view.

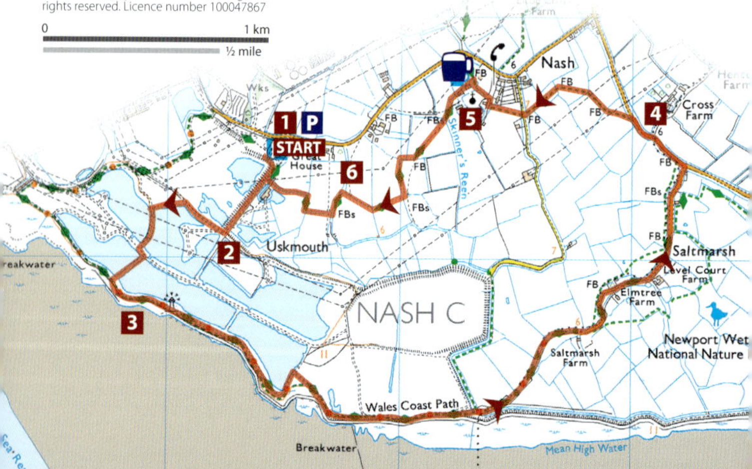

Approaching the Newport Wetlands visitor centre

Turn left onto the coast path towards the stumpy **East Usk lighthouse**.

East Usk lighthouse marks the eastern side of the Usk estuary. Its partner on the west side is also visible from here. Both are still used to help ships navigate into Newport Docks, along with the red and green buoys marking the channel. The lighthouse was once taller than it is now – the level of the land increased as ash from the power station was tipped here.

3. Continue past the lighthouse, and shortly after the path bears to the left and continues ahead, follow the **Wales Coast Path** to the right. Continue on the Coast Path until you reach a lane at **Saltmarsh Farm**.

Follow the lane to **Goldcliff Road**. Turn left and follow this road around a couple of blind bends. Although this is a quiet road, please walk so you are visible to oncoming traffic.

4. About 20 metres from the last bend, cross the **bridge** on the left with stiles at each end. This is the first of a **series of bridges** with gates or stiles at both ends, crossing the drainage ditches that punctuate this low-lying land. From the bridge, take a diagonal right, heading past wind turbines to another bridge.

A coastal track runs between the saltmarsh and the inland reedbeds

Follow the edge of the next field, then cross another stile. Take a diagonal left across the next field to another **footbridge**.

Now head straight over the field to the corner of the hedge, then keep the hedge on your left to the next **bridge**. Cross the road and **another bridge**. Take a diagonal right towards the church. The exit point in the corner of the field is not visible until you are close. Walk around the **church** to the **pub**.

5. On leaving the pub, turn left and then left again across the small **parking area**. In the far corner, cross the **bridge** and turn left to follow the path immediately behind the **pub garden**.

You are now back on the **Wales Coast Path,** and the route back to the nature reserve is well signposted.

Cross the gate at the end of the field and continue straight ahead until the drainage ditch veers left. Take a diagonal left to the next **bridge**. Follow the signs diagonally right to the far side of the field, then diagonally left to a wooden gate only about 20 metres away.

Cross the **bridge**. Follow the field boundary on the left. At the field gate directly ahead, bear right over another **wooden bridge**. Turn right along the drainage ditch, crossing a **series of bridges** until you reach a stone track.